Stay with Me, Lord

"It is not uncommon for prayer to seem impossible. Let Padre Pio be your spiritual director! Pio was not only a spiritual master but a faithful priest, sought after for his deep devotion to being an instrument of Divine Mercy in the Sacrament of Reconciliation. He knew suffering in his own mind, body, and soul and in his fellow traveling humans. This book is one for our day. The time is now to start praying, knowing it is often the greatest and most practical action we can take in the face of the overwhelming."

Kathryn Jean Lopez
Religion editor of *National Review* magazine
and senior fellow at the National Review Institute

"People see the miracles of Padre Pio, but he was purified by trials, rejected by his own, and misunderstood by many. He overcame these daily trials by repeating the humble plea 'Stay with me, Lord.' His heart was a burning furnace of love. If you struggle—falling again and again—yet deeply ache for your heart to burn with that same divine love, Padre Pio can help. Through his intimate letters in this book, he speaks directly to that longing: a flame of living love that invades the soul, burns away distractions and illusions, and leaves us desiring God even more intensely.

"Padre Pio's witness shows that even in weakness, dryness, or repeated stumbles, the Lord's gentle fire purifies, delights, and draws us closer. Let these thirty days of reflections, prayers, and Padre Pio's own words accompany you: Stay with him, and watch your heart slowly catch fire."

Fr. Agustino Torres, CFR
Founder of Corazón Puro

Stay with Me, Lord

GREAT SPIRITUAL TEACHERS

30 DAYS WITH

Padre Pio

With Susan De Bartoli

Ave Maria Press AVE Notre Dame, Indiana

Scripture quotations are taken from the *New Revised Standard Version Bible: Catholic Edition*, copyright © 1989, 1993 the Division of Christian Education of the National Council of the Churches of Christ in the United States of America. Used by permission. All rights reserved.

"My Day Begins" sections are excerpted from Padre Pio, *Letters I: Correspondence with His Spiritual Directors (1910–1922)*, Edizioni Padre Pio da Pietrelcina, 2011. All rights reserved.

The following sections are written by Susan De Bartoli: "Timeline," "Who Is Padre Pio," "All Through the Day," and "My Day Is Ending."

Series editor: John Kirvan

 Ave Maria Press®, Inc., P.O. Box 428, Notre Dame, IN 46556, 1-800-282-1865.

Founded in 1865, Ave Maria Press is a ministry of the United States Province of Holy Cross.

www.avemariapress.com

Paperback: ISBN-13 978-1-64680-472-6

E-book: ISBN-13 978-1-64680-473-3

Cover image © Meyer Market Designs, Bernadette Meyer.

Cover and text design by Katherine Robinson Coleman.

Printed and bound in the United States of America.

Contents

Timeline

1887	May 25: Francesco Forgione is born in Pietrelcina (Benevento) to Grazio Forgione and Maria Giuseppa (Peppa) Di Nunzio.
	May 26: Francesco is baptized in the church of Sant'Anna.
1903	January 6: Francesco enters the novitiate of the Capuchins in Morcone.
	January 22: Francesco takes the habit of the Capuchin order and the name of Brother Pio.
1907	January 27: Brother Pio takes his final vows.
1910	August 10: Brother Pio is ordained a priest in the cathedral of Benevento.
	August 14: Padre Pio says his first Mass in Pietrelcina.
1911	September 8: Padre Pio suffers from pains in his hands and feet; he reveals to his spiritual adviser, Padre Benedetto from San Marco in Lamis,

	that he has had the "invisible stigmata for about a year."
1915	October 10: Padre Pio tells his superior that he has been suffering the pain inflicted by flagellations and the crowning of thorns for years.
1916	February 17: Padre Pio is appointed to the Monastery of Sant'Anna in Foggia.
	July 28: During a period of suffocating heat, he is taken to the Monastery of San Giovanni Rotondo and stays there one week.
	December 18: Padre Pio goes to Naples for national military service, but his poor physical condition makes the doctors send him home on special leave.
1917	November 12: Padre Pio returns to the Monastery of San Giovanni Rotondo, where he stays until March 5, 1918, the date he resumes military service in Naples.

1918	March 16: Padre Pio returns to the Monastery of San Giovanni Rotondo for good.
	August 5: Padre Pio's heart is pierced by a spear by a mysterious celestial being, leaving him with a wound that was to bleed for the rest of his life. This phenomenon is known as "transverberation."
	September 20: Padre Pio's body is marked with stigmata, the visible signs of the Passion of Christ.
1919	News of Padre Pio's stigmata spreads throughout Italy, and thousands of pilgrims, attracted by this charismatic figure, begin to make their way to the Gargano.
	May 15: The first examination of Padre Pio's stigmata is done by Professor Luigi Romanelli, a doctor and consultant at the hospital of Barletta.
	July 26: Padre Pio is examined by Professor Amico Bignami, head of the

medical pathology department at the Sapienza University of Rome.

October 9: At the request of the general of the Capuchins, Padre Venanzio from Lisle-en-Rigault, Padre Pio undergoes in-depth medical examinations conducted by Dr. Giorgio Festa.

1923 June 23: Padre Pio is debarred from saying Mass in public or replying to any of the letters arriving at the Monastery of San Giovanni Rotondo.

June 25: A revolt breaks out on the afternoon of the day when Padre Pio first says Mass in a private chapel.

June 26: Padre Pio resumes saying Mass in the church.

August 8: Padre Pio is ordered to move to Ancona.

1925 April 22: The faithful throughout the country, resenting the restrictions placed on Padre Pio's confessional duties, are again in a state of turmoil.

1933	July 16: Padre Pio resumes saying Mass in public following a two-year suspension.
1940	January 9: Work starts on Padre Pio's Casa Sollievo della Sofferenza (House for the Relief of Suffering).
1956	May 5: Casa Sollievo della Sofferenza is officially opened.
1968	September 22: Padre Pio says Mass at 5 a.m. as usual. This is his last celebration of the Eucharist.
	September 23: Padre Pio dies at 2:30 a.m. His last words are "Jesus, Mary! Jesus, Mary!"
	September 26: Over one hundred thousand people attend his funeral.
	September 27: The crypt containing Padre Pio's body is opened to the public; over the years, pilgrims have continued to visit it.
1983	March 20: The official inquiry into Padre Pio's case is opened in San Giovanni Rotondo.

1987	May 23: The Holy Father, Pope John Paul II, makes a pilgrimage to San Giovanni Rotondo and prays at Padre Pio's tomb.
1990	January 21: The investigation is completed, and Padre Pio is declared a Servant of God.
1997	December 18: Padre Pio is declared Venerable.
1999	May 2: Padre Pio of Pietrelcina is beatified by Pope John Paul II.
2002	June 16: Padre Pio of Pietrelcina is canonized by Pope John Paul II and given the name St. Pio of Pietrelcina.
2004	July 1: The new Sanctuary of Saint Pio of Pietrelcina is consecrated in San Giovanni Rotondo.

WHO IS

Padre Pio?

To a world that often doubts the supernatural, the life of Padre Pio stands as a radiant contradiction, challenging modern skepticism not with spectacle or self-promotion but through the quiet, powerful force of holiness lived to its fullest. He was not a man of grand gestures or attention-seeking public displays. He was, instead, a relentless warrior for good, a mystic hidden in the folds of humility, and a living crucifix who bore the wounds of Christ in both body and soul. His sanctity was sacrificial. And it began before he could speak a word.

When asked when the attacks from the forces of darkness began, Padre Pio responded with a simplicity that stunned even the devout: "In my mother's womb." With those few words, he revealed the extraordinary nature of his vocation. He was a soul anointed from the beginning for battle, called to carry the weight of suffering for the salvation of others. His was not a symbolic struggle. It was literal, painful, and relentless. Yet in every trial, he chose surrender over resistance, silence over spectacle, and prayer over despair.

Francesco Forgione was born on May 25, 1887, in the small hamlet of Pietrelcina, Italy. His early life was simple and humble. Although he experienced visits from Jesus, the Blessed Virgin Mary, and angels from a young age, Francesco never considered himself special. As a child, he assumed that all children were graced with such heavenly visits.

At the age of eight, Francesco was taken out of school to help his family by tending sheep in the fields. While grazing the flock, he devoted himself to prayer, especially in a place called Piana Romana. There, the family owned a modest one-room house used for midday meals and shelter from the *mezzogiorno,* the intense noonday sun. It was also where they rested during their afternoon siesta before returning to the fields. Outside this small house stood a beautiful elm tree under which Francesco would sit for hours, reciting countless Rosaries.

Those who knew Francesco described him as a deeply holy child, constantly immersed in prayer. He prayed the Rosary throughout the day while in the fields and again at home with his family. The rosary became his most treasured possession. When not tending sheep, he was often found in church, speaking to Jesus in the Tabernacle. Above all, he held a special love for the Christ Child.

Starting in October each year, while in the fields, Francesco would gather bits of clay from the earth and begin sculpting nativity figures in preparation for Advent. When it came time to shape the Christ Child, he would repeatedly mold and reshape it until it matched the image in his heart. As Francesco grew, so did his devotion. When he received his First Communion and Confirmation in 1899 at the age of twelve, he knew in his heart that he was called to be a priest. Through prayer, he discerned that he was to become a Capuchin friar. This calling had been evident since the age of five when he had already consecrated his life to God.

One day at the age of fifteen, while praying about his vocation, Francesco experienced an event that changed the course of his life. He saw a majestic figure, as radiant as the sun. Francesco called him "the Guide." This Guide led him to a field where two groups stood, one clothed in black, the other in white. The Guide asked him if he was willing to defend the Lord. When he said yes, a towering demon appeared, so vast its head touched the clouds.

At the sight of this demon, Francesco felt his life suspended. He turned pale, trembled all over, and was on the point of falling to the ground in a faint, so great was his terror. But the Guide assured him he would not be alone. Despite believing he might die, Francesco fought and defeated the demon.

As a reward, the Guide placed a dazzling crown on his head, only to remove it and promise that a far greater one awaited him in heaven. From that moment on, Francesco no longer felt part of this world; he felt his life was not his own. He would spend the rest of it defending the Lord and fighting demons until the day of his death.

In September of 1910, after his ordination, Padre Pio received the stigmata for the first time while praying under the elm tree in Piana Romana. Jesus himself bestowed this sacred gift upon him. Padre Pio humbly accepted the invitation to suffer for Christ but prayed that the wounds would remain hidden from the world. His prayer was answered, and the stigmata became invisible, remaining so until September 20, 1918, when it became visible again.

Padre Pio was an extraordinary man with many extraordinary gifts. Those closest to him attested to seeing those gifts made manifest long before the appearance of the stigmata, as early as when he first entered the seminary. These events were recorded on the seal of testimony by Padre Pio's superiors, and some of these gifts were not revealed until after his death, during the investigation for his cause for sainthood.

Among the spiritual and mystical charisms of the Holy Spirit attributed to Padre Pio are the gifts of healing, bilocation, levitation, prophecy, miracles, extraordinary abstinence from both sleep and nourishment, the ability to read hearts, the gift of tongues, the gift of conversions, the gift of tears, and the fragrance of holiness (emanating from his wounds).

Following World War II, Padre Pio's name began to spread far beyond southern Italy. Returning soldiers spoke of miraculous encounters. Some claimed he had protected them in battle; others described experiences in the confessional that revealed the hidden depths of their hearts. A few gave up everything to follow Christ after meeting him. Through the power of these testimonies, and with the support of these soldiers, Padre Pio's dream was realized: A hospital was built in San Giovanni Rotondo, a haven of healing born from faith and sacrifice.

His message to the world was disarmingly simple: "Pray, hope, and don't worry." These were not comforting platitudes; they were words forged in fire, born from a life lived face-to-face with evil and anchored in unshakeable trust in God.

Padre Pio showed that sanctity is not reserved for the extraordinary but cultivated through ordinary daily faithfulness, moment by moment, in prayer, obedience, and self-offering. It is shaped in silence and proven in suffering.

To truly understand Padre Pio, one must go beyond the miracles and meet the man: the confessor who spent hours reconciling souls to God; the priest who offered each Mass as though he were standing at Calvary itself; and the spiritual father who comforted, corrected, and carried others in prayer. His life was a continuous act of intercession. He didn't merely pray for others; he bore their crosses.

In everything he did, Padre Pio pointed away from himself and toward Christ. He led countless souls to Christ and invited them to drink deeply from the well of divine mercy. His prayer life, his fasting, his love for the Blessed Mother, and his passionate devotion to the Rosary were all expressions of a heart that belonged entirely to Jesus.

At the heart of his devotion was a single, piercing longing: that Christ would never leave him. So profound was this desire that he composed a prayer to be said after Mass: "Stay with Me, Lord." In it, we hear the cry of a soul that could not bear to be apart from its Savior. It is a prayer of intimacy, of dependence, and of surrender, and it captures the very essence of who Padre Pio was. That prayer serves as the inspiration for this book.

Padre Pio is not merely a saint of the past. He is a spiritual guide for the present and a signpost for the future. In a world starving for truth, beauty, and meaning, his life calls out with clarity and compassion. He teaches us that holiness is possible even now. And he reminds us that no suffering, however great, is wasted when united to Christ.

As you turn these pages, may you encounter not only the legacy of a remarkable man but also the living presence of a saint who still walks beside us, still intercedes for us, and gave us the words that can change our lives: "Stay with me, Lord."

Stay with Me, Lord

PADRE PIO WROTE THIS PRAYER AND PRAYED IT AFTER COMMUNION.

Stay with me, Lord, for it is necessary
to have you present so that I do not forget you.
You know how easily I abandon you.
Stay with me, Lord, because I am weak
and I need your strength, that I may not fall so often.
Stay with me, Lord, for you are my life,
and without you, I am without meaning and hope.
Stay with me, Lord, for you are my light,
and without you, I am in darkness.
Stay with me, Lord, to show me your will.
Stay with me, Lord, so that I can hear your voice
and follow you.
Stay with me, Lord, for I desire to love you
ever more, and to be in your company always.
Stay with me, Lord, if you wish me to be
faithful to you.

Stay with me, Lord, for as poor as my soul is,
I wish it to be a place of consolation for you,
a dwelling of your love.
Stay with me, Jesus, for it is getting late;
the days are coming to a close, and life is passing.
Death, judgment, eternity are drawing near.
It is necessary to renew my strength
so that I will not stop along the way,
and for that, I need you.
It is getting late and death approaches.
I fear the darkness, the temptations, the dryness,
the cross, the sorrows.
O, how I need you, my Jesus, in this night of exile!
Stay with me, Jesus, because in the darkness of life,
with all its dangers, I need you.
Help me to recognize you as your disciples did
at the breaking of the bread,
so that the Eucharistic Communion be the Light
which disperses the darkness,
the power which sustains me,
the unique joy of my heart.
Stay with me, Lord, because at the hour
of my death, I want to be one with you,

and if not by communion,
at least by your grace and love.
Stay with me, Jesus; I do not ask for
divine consolations because I do not deserve them,
but I only ask for the gift of your presence.
Oh yes, I ask this of you!
Stay with me, Lord, for I seek you alone,
your Love, your Grace, your Will, your Heart,
your Spirit, because I love you, and I ask no other
reward but to love you more and more
with a strong and active love.
Grant that I may love you with all my heart
while on earth so that I can continue to love you
perfectly throughout all eternity, dear Jesus.
Amen!

HOW TO
Use This Book

The books in the Great Spiritual Teachers series provide an introduction to the spiritual insights and wisdom of some of history's most extraordinary saints. Through these pages, you're invited to a place beyond mere reading, into an experience of daily prayer and meditation. You'll be accompanied by a spiritual teacher whose wisdom will awaken, enrich, and empower your walk with the Lord.

In other words, these books take you on a spiritual journey.

We have some suggestions for how you can make the most of this journey. But keep in mind that these books are meant to help you experience the freedom and joy of communing with God in prayer. The daily format is there to help—but don't hesitate to go at your own pace or take your own route! Repeat a day as often as you like, or skip a day if the reading isn't resonating with where you are in your journey. The goal is to hear the voice of God through the words of the saints.

However you choose to use this book, it's helpful to understand the thinking behind the format used for each day. We've chosen to follow the suggestion of the classic book on spirituality *The Cloud of Unknowing,* which describes a three-part movement of *reading, reflecting,* and *praying*: "These three are so linked together that there can be no profitable reflection without first reading or hearing. Nor will beginners or even the spiritually adept come to true prayer without first taking time to reflect on what they have heard or read."

Throughout these thirty days, you'll follow in the footsteps of this long-standing tradition. Each day starts with a section called "My Day Begins," in which you'll find a passage quoted or adapted from a great spiritual teacher. This is followed by "All Through the Day," which provides a short, memorable phrase (drawn from or based on the reading) that you can carry with you throughout the day, enabling you to reflect and meditate on a key truth, question, or insight. In the final section, "My Day Is Ending," you're encouraged to find a quiet place to go to the Lord in prayer, drawing on that day's reading as you lift up your petitions and praises to him.

My Day Begins

One of the best ways you can begin your day is to put yourself in the company of a great spiritual teacher.

The selected passages are short—just a few hundred words. But they are powerful! They've been chosen specifically for their ability to provide spiritual focus for your day and to remind you that you are a spiritual being, intended for relationship and intimacy with God.

These morning readings don't just put you in the presence of a spiritual teacher who can accompany you on your journey—they are also designed to invite you into God's presence so you can start your day in conversation with him.

If you find that you don't fully understand the reading, don't be discouraged! Understanding may come with time, meditation, and further prayer. For now, focus on your heart's response. Tell the Lord about the questions you have, and ask him for wisdom and insight.

It's also helpful to read *slowly*. We've divided the passages into sense lines to help you do just that. Instead of rushing through the reading, savor each word. Pay attention to which phrases or images resonate in your heart. Make room for God to speak. In short, read prayerfully. Each day's opening reading is meant to foster attentiveness to God and an attitude of readiness to hear what he wants to say to you.

All Through the Day

After the day's reading, you'll find a single sentence, a meditation that you can reflect on throughout your day. As you move forward with the busyness of everyday life, return to this reflection as often as you can. Try writing it down on a card and placing it somewhere you'll see it frequently. Or copy it down in a journal or planner. Recite it in the little free moments between tasks and conversations.

This reflection shouldn't take you out of the day's responsibilities; rather, it should serve as a gentle reminder of God's presence within the many activities and tasks that make up your day—and an expression of your desire to live in connection with him.

My Day Is Ending

No matter what your day has brought to you, there's great wisdom in reaching the end of it and turning everything over to God in prayer, intentionally setting your mind and heart on him, and listening for his voice.

If you find that it's not easy to let go of the events of the day, to find peace and closure and solace in God's presence, here are some suggestions to help you:

1. Find a quiet, distraction-free place that you can return to each evening.
2. Quiet your spirit. Sometimes this involves relaxing your body and letting go of physical tension. Try adopting a posture that reminds you that you are in God's presence: Sit or kneel; fold your hands or lift them up—whatever works for you. Focus on breathing deeply and deliberately.
3. When you feel calm and at peace, focus on the evening prayer phrase by phrase. If you find yourself getting caught up in analyzing the words of the prayer, wrestling with the meaning of a phrase, or becoming distracted, don't worry! Just pause, breathe, and begin again. Set aside all the distractions and worries that stand between you and God.

The time spent with the evening prayer doesn't need to be very long—just remember that it is a time of expressing complete trust and confidence in God, preparing yourself for a night of peaceful sleep. End the day as you began it, resting in his presence.

Some Other Ways to Use This Book

1. *Create your own reflections.* If the provided "All Through the Day" reflection doesn't resonate with you, or if you'd like to add to it, feel free to choose another phrase or image from the morning reading that caught your attention.
2. *Incorporate journaling into your spiritual journey.* Many find that journaling—either through copying out the provided reflections and prayers or writing your own—is an excellent way to slow down and focus, ensuring that your mind doesn't skip over important insights. Or you could use a journal to keep a record of your experiences on this thirty-day journey, such as the insights that had the biggest impact on your thinking, or any daily changes you noticed in your heart or behavior.
3. *Look for contrasts.* Sometimes two readings or reflections might seem to stand in tension with each other. Often, such tensions highlight areas

for fruitful reflection. Write down the contrasting passages and any questions they raise. Meditate on them and pray about them—God may provide new illumination as you ponder!

4. *Form a small group.* You're not alone in seeking to deepen your spiritual life—so why not invite others to join you on your thirty-day journey with a great spiritual teacher? Try meeting weekly—whether over coffee or over a shared meal—to discuss that week's readings, reflections, and prayers. Talk to each other about how God is working in your lives. Pray together.

We hope that you'll be richly blessed by the books in this series. As you intentionally fill your days with the words and wisdom of a great spiritual teacher, we pray that you'll be ushered daily into the divine presence, experiencing more deeply than ever the life-giving joy of intimacy with the God who loves you.

The Publisher

THIRTY DAYS WITH

Padre Pio

DAY 1

My Day Begins

LETTER TO NINA
CAMPANILE, A TEACHER

Dear God! Who can describe the martyrdom I went through in my inmost? Even the memory of that internal combat makes the blood freeze in my veins, although almost twenty years have passed since then, when I heard the voice of duty telling me to obey you, O true and good God! But your enemies and mine tyrannized over me. They dislocated my bones; they mocked me and caused me to writhe in agony.

All Through the Day

Pray, hope, and don't worry.

My Day Is Ending

Stay with me, Lord,
as I reflect on the life of your servant, Padre Pio,
whose heart burned with love for you
and sorrow for souls far from you.
You called him to be a living sacrifice,
a vessel of light, warmth,
and healing through suffering.
Though he could not see the full path ahead,
he trusted your will and surrendered all.

You drew him into your Passion,
molding him in silence until the wounds of love
marked his body.
He bore them humbly, offering his pain for others.

Lord Jesus, as I contemplate his path,
I ask you:
What are you asking of my heart?
How are you inviting me to share
in my own small way
in the sufferings of Christ?

Teach me to offer my life, too,
as a gift for the healing of the world,
for the salvation of souls,
and for the glory of your holy name.

May I embrace the cross you give me
not with fear but with love.
May my trials, united with yours,
become prayer.
May my wounds, offered with trust,
become grace.

May my life, like his, reflect your light
for the healing of souls and the hope of the world.

Amen.

DAY 2

My Day Begins

*LETTERS, SEPTEMBER 4, 1910;
NOVEMBER 29, 1910; AND MAY 27, 1915*

By God's will I still continue in very poor health. But what torments me most of all are the severe pains in my chest. At times these are so violent that it seems they must split my back and chest.

My cough is so severe and continual, especially during the night, that it almost splits my chest, and I am frequently so afraid that I say the Act of Contrition.

For several days I have been afflicted by severe headaches, which make it impossible for me to concentrate on anything.

All Through the Day

At Jesus's feet, I rest and regain my strength.

My Day Is Ending

Stay with me, Lord,
as this day draws to a close.
Worry drains the soul and serves no purpose,
so I lay it down before you now.
You are merciful and ever loving,
close to the brokenhearted
and attentive to every whispered prayer,
even those too deep for words.

In your presence, I find peace.

Let me not only hear your voice but also
feel the beating of your heart within it.
Unite my heart to yours, Lord.
Speak to me through the silence,
especially when the night grows long and heavy.

Teach me to walk through every dark valley
not with fear but with trust,
knowing that you are guiding each step I take.

Teach me to trust you completely,
even when the road ahead is hidden.
To believe that every night will yield to morning,
and every sorrow holds a seed of joy.

Teach us, Lord, to speak to you
not only with words
but with hearts wide open.
Sometimes, the most powerful prayers are silent,
where only love speaks.

So here in my silence, in my weariness,
and in my longing,
hear my heart, Lord.

Lead me through this night
with the light of hope before me.
Fill me with courage to wait upon you
so that I may arrive at a day with no more sorrow,
no more tears,
only everlasting peace in your presence.

Amen.

DAY 3

My Day Begins

LETTER, SEPTEMBER 20, 1912

I feel within me the great need to cry out louder and louder to Jesus with the doctor of grace: "Give me what you command and command what you will." Hence my dear Father, do not allow the idea of my sufferings to cast a shadow on your spirit or to sadden your heart. So let's not weep, my dear Father; we must hide our tears from the One who sends them, from the One who has shed tears himself and continues to shed them every day because of man's ingratitude. He chooses souls, and despite my unworthiness, he has chosen mine also to help him in the tremendous task of men's salvation.

The more these souls suffer without the slightest consolation, the more the sufferings of our good Jesus are alleviated.

This is the whole reason that I desire to suffer more and more without the slightest consolation.

All Through the Day

He has chosen me to help him.

My Day Is Ending

Stay with me, Lord,
for I desire not only your comfort
but that I myself become a comfort to you.
Strengthen me with your presence
so that my heart will not wound yours again.

Let me share in your darkness
so that your own sorrow
may be made lighter by my love.

Show me your will.
Let me love it, accept it,
and live it in silence and humility.

Let me hear your voice
even in the storms of my heart,
and follow it without hesitation.

I wish my poor soul
to be a place of rest for you—
a small, quiet dwelling
where you may find consolation
from the ingratitude of the world.

Let me not seek relief for myself
but offer every pain to you
as a balm for your Sacred Heart.

Strengthen me for the final journey
so that I may walk faithfully with you
unto the end.

Then, whether in joy or suffering,
my own consolation will be this:
that I have been a consolation to you.

Amen.

DAY 4

My Day Begins

LETTER, DECEMBER 29, 1912

Oh, Jesus, if I could only love you, if I could only suffer as much as I should in order to make you happy and make some kind of reparation for humanity's ingratitude toward you.

But Jesus made his voice more clearly audible in my heart: "My son, love is recognized as suffering; you will feel it acutely in your soul and even more acutely in your body."

My dear Father, to me these words remain very obscure.

Those demons are trying to torment me in every way; I complained to Jesus of this, and I hear him say to me, "Courage! After the battle comes peace."

He tells me I must be faithful and courageous. I am ready for anything as long as I am doing his will.

All Through the Day

Jesus, I offer my love, my suffering, and my life to you.

My Day Is Ending

Stay with me, Lord.
You have taught us through scripture, the saints,
and the whisper of your Spirit
that time is a gift, and every moment is sacred
when lived for your glory.
You surrendered each breath to the Father's will;
help me to follow you with that same devotion.
Let me see my days not as burdens to endure
but as offerings of love returned to you.

Stay with me, Lord.
Help me to see suffering not as wasted pain
but as a sacred opportunity to love more deeply.
You did not glorify pain, but you transformed it,
and when united with your Cross,
even my trials can become redemptive.

Strengthen me by your Spirit,
your very life within me,
to walk each step with courage and faith.
Remind me that nothing done for you is ever lost,
even in the hidden, ordinary moments.
You see it all. You receive it all.

May every heartbeat echo with surrender.
May every breath proclaim your goodness.
And whether seen or unseen,
may my life shine only with your light.

Amen.

DAY 5

My Day Begins

LETTER, FEBRUARY 1, 1913

When Jesus wants to make me understand that he loves me, he permits me to relish the wounds, the thorns, the anguish of his passion. When he wants me to rejoice, he fills my heart with that spirit that is all fire, and he speaks to me of his delights. But when he wants to be delighted, he speaks to me of his sufferings; he invites me in a tone that is both a request and a command to offer my body that his suffering may be alleviated.

All Through the Day

I will lay my life down for you, my Lord.

My Day Is Ending

Stay with me, Lord,
and let me love you not only in joy and consolation
but in silence, in suffering,
and in the dryness of spirit.
Let my heart grow in maturity,
like that of your servant Padre Pio,
who longed to love you not for reward
but simply because you are worthy of all love.

Lord, I bring before you my moments of regret,
times I have forgotten you, wandered from you,
or failed to respond to your grace.
Yet I do not remain in sorrow.
Let my awareness of weakness awaken in me
a deeper longing for your mercy,
a greater desire to love you with all that I am.

In the quiet seasons, when your voice seems still,
remind me that your love remains unchanged.
Teach me to embrace silence not as absence
but as a sacred space where my love for you can grow
stripped of emotion, sustained by faith alone.

Stay with me, Lord,
and let my love be shown not only in words
but in patience when I am weary,
in endurance when I feel alone,
in sacrifice when I must let go,
and in faithfulness when the road is long.

Let every moment, whether joyful or painful,
become an offering of love to you,
who loved me first, and never stops loving.

Amen.

DAY 6

My Day Begins

LETTER, NOVEMBER 8, 1916

I beseech you, oh my good God, to be my life, my ship, and my port. You have placed me on the Cross of your Son, and I am trying to accustom myself to it as best I can. I am convinced that I shall never come down from that Cross and that I shall never again see a clear sky.

All Through the Day

I love you, Jesus. Be my safe place.

My Day Is Ending

Stay with me, Lord.
Be my life, my source and strength.
Be my ship, the vessel that carries me
through every storm.

Be my port, my final rest and eternal home.
I give myself entirely to you,
not in part, but wholly,
with no conditions, no reservations,
no turning back.
You alone are my refuge, my reason, and my reward.
Teach me to accept the cross you place
upon my shoulders
not with resistance but with quiet love.
Let me embrace the trials you permit
not as burdens to escape
but as opportunities to draw closer to your Heart.
Let me see my suffering not as punishment
but as a sharing in your Son's Passion,
a hidden way of redeeming love.

Grant me the grace to endure with patience,
to obey even without understanding,
to remain faithful even when the skies stay clouded
and your voice is silent.

When comfort is absent and clarity fades,
teach me to love you still.
Let my love be real,

a love without reward, without feeling,
pure and persistent in the darkness,
like a lamp burning quietly through the night.
For even when I do not feel peace,
I know you are near.

I entrust to you my entire journey:
past, with all its wounds and wonders;
present, with all its struggles and hopes;
future, with all its unknowns.
Let every step, every sorrow, every joy
be lived in you and for you.

Let my cross become a gift, not a burden,
a sign of love, not of loss.
May my suffering, united to yours,
bear fruit for souls,
bring healing to the broken,
and give glory to your name.

Amen.

DAY 7

My Day Begins

LETTER, NOVEMBER 29, 1910

For some time past, I have felt the need to offer myself to the Lord as a victim for poor sinners and for the souls in purgatory.

This desire has been growing continually in my heart so that it has now become what I would call a strong passion. I have in fact made this offering to the Lord several times, beseeching him to pour out upon me the punishments prepared for sinners and for the souls in a state of purgation, even increasing them a hundredfold for me, as long as he converts and saves sinners and quickly admits to paradise the souls in purgatory.

All Through the Day

I want to feel your troubles as if they were my own.

My Day Is Ending

Stay with me, Lord,
and teach me to embrace my cross
not with fear but with trust.
Give me strength to endure with patience,
to obey without understanding,
and to love without seeking comfort.

You gave yourself completely for love of us,
wounded, crucified, and poured out to save souls.
With a heart full of sorrow for those
who do not know you
and compassion for the holy souls in purgatory,
I come before you with a humble offering.

If it be your will,
take my prayers, my daily trials, my sufferings
and unite them to your Cross.
Let them become instruments of mercy:
for the conversion of poor sinners
and the release of souls longing to see your face.

Burn within me a holy desire to suffer
not for punishment
but for love,
not for recognition
but for redemption.

Above all, Lord,
keep me rooted in obedience,
always discerning through those
you have placed over me,
so that my offering may be pure,
pleasing, and in harmony with your will.

May I never run from suffering
if it means loving you more
and helping even one soul come home.

Jesus, I am yours.
Do with me as you will,
for your glory, for the salvation of souls,
and for the joy of heaven.

Amen.

DAY 8

My Day Begins

LETTERS, NOVEMBER 18, 1912, AND JULY 10, 1914

Jesus, his beloved Mother, the little Angel, and the others continue to encourage me, and they keep on repeating that a victim properly so-called must lose all his blood. To have such a tender Father by one's side in the battle is sweet and consoling.

My soul must endure a continual combat. I see no other way out than to abandon myself in the arms of Jesus where he often allows me to fall asleep. Blessed sleep! Happy refreshment for the soul in the struggles it endures.

All Through the Day

O what a beautiful thing it is to become a victim of love.

My Day Is Ending

Stay with me, Lord.
You call me not only to follow you in joy
but to walk with you along the road of the Cross.
You, who poured out all your blood for love of souls,
invite me to offer myself completely,
not in part but wholly,
for those who do not yet know you,
for sinners, and for the souls in purgatory.

If you desire my life to be a hidden sacrifice,
then take it, Lord, and use it as you will.
Let every wound, sorrow, and burden
become a quiet gift of love in your hands.

Stay with me, Lord, and when the battle
within grows heavy,
when temptations and discouragement press in,
remind me that I am not alone.
Let me feel the nearness of your Mother,
my guardian angel, and all the saints.

Surround me with the strength of heaven
when mine begins to fail.

Invite us, Lord, into the mystery
of redemptive suffering,
through this spiritual battle, to divine consolation.

And when I can fight no longer,
draw me close to your Heart.
Let me fall asleep in your arms,
not in despair, but in holy surrender,
a child resting in the Father's love.

This is enough for me:
to be near you,
to trust you,
to love you in the dark.

Take my life, Lord.
Let it be a vessel of mercy.
Let my hidden sufferings bring light to others.

Amen.

DAY 9

My Day Begins

LETTER, JULY 10, 1915

Peace is simplicity of heart, serenity of mind, tranquility of soul, the bond of love. Peace means order, harmony in our whole being; it means continual contentment springing from the knowledge of a good conscience; it is the holy joy of a heart in which God reigns. Peace is the way to perfection; indeed, in peace is perfection to be found. The devil, who is well aware of all this, makes every effort to have us lose our peace.

All Through the Day

Jesus, you are my peace.

My Day Is Ending

Stay with me, Lord,
to teach me that peace is not just a passing feeling,
but a holy state of the soul,
rooted in your presence.
Grant me the simplicity of heart, serenity of mind,
and tranquility of soul that come only when
you reign within me.
Keep my conscience pure before you.
Help me to live honestly in your sight,
avoiding sin and making amends quickly
when I fall,
so that my heart may rest
without guilt or inner turmoil.

Stay with me, Lord, and bind me in the bond of love,
love for you above all things,
and love for my neighbor as you have loved me.
Let this love cast out fear
and bring unity to all my thoughts,
words, and deeds.
Make my soul good soil for holiness, O Lord.

Let virtue grow in the calm waters of your peace,
and keep me from the agitation and anxiety
that choke the life of the Spirit within me.
When storms rise within or without,
remind me that your peace is stronger
than every wind,
and that no darkness can overcome the light you give.
I know the enemy will try to steal this treasure,
whispering fear, confusion, and temptation.
But I choose to cling to you in every trial.
When peace begins to slip away,
draw me quickly back into your presence
and teach me to trust you completely.

Jesus,
be my peace, my shelter, and my perfection,
now and forever.

Amen.

DAY 10

My Day Begins

LETTER, JUNE 20, 1915

The bitterness of the trial is sweetened by the balm of God's goodness and mercy. Praise be to God, who can so marvelously alternate joy and tears so as to lead the soul by unknown paths to the attainment of perfection, a flower that the merciful God causes to bloom amid the thorns of suffering, watered by the tears of the soul that suffers patiently, that humbly conforms to the divine will and prays with warmth and fervor.

All Through the Day

God's mercy sweetens my trials. He leads me through joy and tears.

My Day Is Ending

Stay with me, Lord,
and remind me that no trial is without meaning.

Even when the road is steep
and the weight is heavy,
your goodness and mercy are at work,
quietly transforming my bitterness
into the sweetness of grace.
When my heart feels the sting of sorrow,
draw near to me and let me recognize your presence
as the balm that heals my wounds.

Teach me to embrace the rhythm
you have written into life,
the alternating seasons of joy and tears,
knowing that both are necessary to shape the soul.
In my joy, keep me from pride;
in my sorrow, keep me from despair.
Let me trust that every tear is counted,
every pain is permitted only so that it may
become a stepping stone toward holiness.

Like a flower blooming among thorns,
let my soul open itself to you in hardship,
finding beauty not in the absence of suffering,
but in the courage to love you through it.

Stay with me, Lord, and make my tears
become living water,
nourishing the seeds of virtue
you have planted within me.
May the thorns that pierce my soul
become the very crown that glorifies you.
And when I am tempted to turn inward in pain,
turn my gaze instead toward you,
my refuge, my strength, my joy, and my reward.

Amen.

DAY 11

My Day Begins

LETTER, AUGUST 25, 1920

What am I to tell you about my spiritual state? It would take too long to tell you, and I lack the time.

I merely ask you to pray and have others pray for me to our good Jesus so that he may accomplish in me, invariably and entirely, his most holy will.

All Through the Day

Jesus, I surrender myself to you; accomplish your will in me.

My Day Is Ending

Stay with me, Lord,
and teach me the humility of Padre Pio,
who sought not to explain himself

but simply to ask for prayer,
that your most holy will might be done in him.

Your will is everything, Lord.
It is my light in darkness,
my compass when I am lost,
my strength when I am weary.
My own plans are small and fragile
beside the greatness of your eternal design.

Stay with me, Lord, and accomplish in me
what you desire,
invariably, entirely, without condition or resistance.

Unite me with the prayers of others,
for I cannot walk this road alone.
In communion with your people,
may I find courage when I am weak,
consolation when I am burdened,
and joy when I am tempted to despair.

Jesus, my Good Shepherd,
I surrender myself completely into your hands.
Guide me through green pastures
and carry me when the road grows steep.

Keep me close to your heart
so that I may never wander from the Father's love.

Grant me patience in waiting,
trust in trial,
and gratitude in every blessing,
for all things come through your providence.
Teach me to embrace each moment as your gift,
whether it brings joy or suffering,
and to rest securely in your care.

Stay with me, Lord, and do with me
what brings glory to the Father,
even if it costs me,
even if I do not understand the path.
I believe, Lord, that you are good,
and that your will leads only to life.

Accomplish in me, O Lord, without fail,
your most holy will—
today, tomorrow, and always.

Amen.

DAY 12

My Day Begins

LETTER, AUGUST 9, 1912

This is just a pallid idea of what Jesus is doing within me. Just as a torrent carries down to the depths of the sea everything it encounters on its way, so also my soul, immersed in the boundless ocean of Jesus's love, by no merit of my own and without my being able to explain it, carries all its treasures along with it.

All Through the Day

Jesus, carry me in the ocean of your love.

My Day Is Ending

Stay with me, Lord,
for I confess that my words are poor.
I cannot grasp the fullness of your work

or the greatness of what you are doing in my soul,
for it is beyond my understanding.
You carry me into the depths
of your boundless love.

Like a torrent rushing to the sea,
take all that I am, my joys, my wounds,
my prayers, my burdens, my hopes,
and even my fears,
and immerse them in the vast ocean of your mercy.

Let nothing of me remain outside of you,
for in you alone I am complete, whole, and at rest.

I know this is not by my merit, Lord,
but only by the gift of your grace.
Keep me humble, keep me grateful,
for everything comes from you and returns to you.

Even when you give only small glimpses,
a star's ray, a flower's fragrance,
a melody's beauty, or the caress of the wind,
teach me to recognize these
as signs of your presence;

gentle reminders that you are near
and attentive to my heart.

Stay with me, Lord, for you are both
mystery and intimacy,
beyond words yet closer than breath.
Draw me ever deeper into yourself,
until I am lost in your love and found only in you.

Amen.

DAY 13

My Day Begins

LETTERS, OCTOBER 10, 1916

Don't be worried by the thought that the time of trial will continue for a long time. Purgatory suffered according to God's will is better than enjoyment of the cloister, a pale image of the heavenly Jerusalem. We don't reach salvation without crossing the stormy sea continually threatened with disaster.

Calvary is the hill of the saints, but from there we pass on to another mountain, which is called Tabor.

All Through the Day

Take heart and have no fear.

My Day Is Ending

Stay with me, Lord,
and teach me not to be anxious
when trials stretch long
and feel heavy upon my shoulders.

In your hands, even purgatory-like suffering,
when endured in love and obedience
to the Father's will,
becomes more precious than all the comforts
the world can offer.

Stay with me, Lord, and teach me to see my pain
not as wasted
but as a hidden seed of redemption,
united to your Cross for the salvation of souls.

This life, with all its fleeting joys,
is only a pale shadow of the heavenly Jerusalem.
Even the peace of holy places,
the beauty of sacred silence,
cannot compare with the glory that awaits
in your presence.

Keep my heart fixed on that promise
so that I do not cling to passing things
but long always for what is eternal.

You remind me, Lord, that life is like a stormy sea:
uncertain, dangerous, and often frightening.
Yet you are the one who calms the waves
and steadies the ship.

Help me to persevere with courage,
remembering that no saint has reached heaven
without crossing through storms.
The road of sacrifice is the path of all who love you.
Beyond Calvary shines Tabor,
the mountain of light and transfiguration.

Teach me to embrace the Cross
with patience and hope,
knowing that every trial borne with you
leads to glory.

Strengthen me, O Lord, to walk this path without fear,
from Calvary to Tabor,
from the storm to the eternal calm of your love.

Amen.

DAY 14

My Day Begins

LETTER, SEPTEMBER 5, 1918

I want to believe at all cost in holy obedience. . . . But I see that this voice of obedience is drowned in the tempest of anxieties and torments, and after the momentary comfort this voice brings, my soul seems to be plunged into a more merciless anguish than before and drinks, in great droughts, the bitter chalice, bereft of all comfort and not knowing why or for whom it is suffering.

All Through the Day

In the storm, I choose obedience.

My Day Is Ending

Stay with me, Lord,
and teach me, like Padre Pio,

even when my heart hesitates in uncertainty,
to let my will cling firmly to you in surrender.

True obedience is found not in comfort or in ease
but in saying yes when confusion clouds the soul
and in trusting you when consolation is absent.

When the storm of anxieties rages within me
and fleeting moments of peace vanish
into deeper anguish,
remind me that this, too,
is part of your purifying work.

Let me not mistake the absence of comfort
for the absence of your presence.

Instead, help me to see that you are at work
in the silence,
drawing me closer, stripping me of self-reliance,
and teaching me to rest in you alone.

If you call me to drink great drafts
of the bitter chalice,
bereft of understanding,
let me embrace it with patience and humility.

For in that chalice, I meet you, Lord, in Gethsemane,
obedient unto death, yet perfectly faithful
to the Father's will.

Stay with me, Lord,
and show me how to unite my small sufferings
to your great sacrifice.
Make my obedience fruitful, even when hidden.
May every act of trust in trial draw me nearer
to your Sacred Heart,
where true peace and eternal joy abide.

Amen.

DAY 15

My Day Begins

LETTER, NOVEMBER 20, 1921

I am consumed by love for God and love for my neighbor. God is continually fixed in my mind and imprinted on my heart. I never lose sight of him. I have to admire his beauty, his benevolence, the agitation he causes, and his mercies, his vengeance, or rather the severity of his justice.

With all this privation of my freedom, with this binding of my faculties both spiritual and corporal, you may imagine the sentiments that consume my poor soul.

Please believe me, Father, when I tell you that my occasional outbursts are caused precisely by this harsh prison, even if you like to call it a happy one.

All Through the Day

Bound by your love, O Lord, I am free.

My Day Is Ending

Stay with me, Lord.
You have seized my soul with your love.
Like Padre Pio, let me feel the fire
of your presence,
a love that consumes,
a love that will not let go,
a love that transforms all weakness into strength.

Stay with me, Lord, and remain fixed in my mind,
imprinted upon my heart.
Your beauty, your mercy,
even the weight of your justice,
all surround me in unceasing contemplation.
I cannot escape you, nor do I wish to,
for even in the struggle, you are my joy,
the song that never fades,
the light that never dims.

Yet this nearness feels at times
like a prison of love,
binding my heart, tying all my thoughts
and actions to you.

It is heavy, Lord, yet holy,
a captivity that both exhausts and exalts,
that empties me so you may fill me with yourself.

When I cry out in weariness,
it is not from lack of love
but from the strain of being held so tightly
by your hand.
Stay with me, Lord,
and teach me to call this prison "happy,"
for it is wrought by your mercy
and secured by your embrace.

O Divine Captor of my soul,
hold me fast in this holy bondage,
until the fire of your love burns away
all that is not you,
and I rest forever in your freedom.

Amen.

DAY 16

My Day Begins

LETTER, AUGUST 10, 1911

I have noticed in myself for several days now an inexplicable spiritual happiness. I am unaware of the cause of this. I no longer experience the great difficulty I had formerly in resigning myself to God's will. In fact, I drive away the tempter's slanderous attacks with such ease that I feel neither annoyed nor wearied. But is this a good or a bad sign? It crosses my mind that the reason for this is a cooling off of my love for God. I leave it to you to imagine how bitter this thought is for me.

In the meantime, nobody but you can rid my mind of these doubts, and you may be sure, dear Father, that I shall not cease to recommend you to the Lord every day, as I have always done. Indeed, I pray for you perhaps more than I do for my own needs.

All Through the Day

Lord, your peace is a gift. May I receive
it with trust.

My Day Is Ending

Stay with me, Lord.
You know the depths of my soul
better than I do myself.
There are moments when you surprise me with joy,
a happiness I did not earn,
a peace that makes surrender to your will
feel light instead of heavy.
And yet, Lord, how quickly my heart
is tempted by doubt!

I wonder if this means I have grown lukewarm,
if the absence of struggle is a sign of lesser love.

But I remember, Lord, that every grace
comes from you.
Sometimes you strengthen me
through trial and struggle,

and sometimes you strengthen me
through consolation and rest.

Both are your gifts, both draw me closer to you.
Stay with me, Lord,
and teach me to trust your work within me,
even when I cannot explain it.

Guard me from suspicion of your love,
and keep me humble enough to seek counsel
and guidance when doubts arise.

Above all, let my heart remain faithful to you,
in dryness or in joy, in light or in shadow,
in weakness or in strength.

Amen.

DAY 17

My Day Begins

LETTERS, MARCH 29, 1911; OCTOBER 14, 1912; AND NOVEMBER 5, 1912

In point of fact, I have to make a great effort to tell you about my affairs. Intense pains in the head almost prevent me from seeing where to place my pen.

This is the war that is being waged on me still. The devil wants the absolute ending of all my relationships and communications with you. He threatens that, if I obstinately refuse to pay attention to him, he will do things to me that the human mind could never conceive.

The new phase of the war is being waged on me by those impure apostates. Since they cannot overcome my fidelity in informing you, dear Father, of their snares, they have had recourse to this other extreme and want to lead me into their nets by depriving me of your counsel through your letters, which are my only comfort. For God's glory and their confusion, I will put up with this.

All Through the Day

Let obedience be my shield, Lord, and your glory my victory.

My Day Is Ending

Stay with me, Lord.
You see how even my body feels the weight
of the battle,
how pain and exhaustion press upon me
in moments of trial.
Yet even in my weakness, you call me to faithfulness.

Stay with me, Lord, and teach me that obedience
and humility are often where the fiercest battles rage.

The enemy seeks to isolate me,
to cut me off from guidance, from encouragement,
from the voices that remind me of your truth.

Temptation thrives in silence and solitude
when I stand alone.
But in obedience, I remain bound to you.

When the devil threatens with fear and confusion,
remind me that his power is nothing
before the Cross.
His torments are shadows;
your light is the reality.
Even when intimidation presses heavily,
your grace is greater still.

Lord, give me the courage to endure for your glory.
Keep me steadfast when trials feel unbearable,
and let my suffering, united to yours,
become a weapon that confuses the enemy
and magnifies your victory.

Jesus, my strength, I trust in you.

Amen.

DAY 18

My Day Begins

LETTERS, JULY 10, 1915, AND DECEMBER 15, 1917

Jesus likes to give himself to simple souls; we must make an effort to acquire this beautiful virtue of simplicity and to hold it in great esteem. Jesus said, "Unless you turn and become like children, you will never enter the kingdom of heaven" (Mt 18:3). We must try to keep our thoughts pure, our ideas upright and honest, and our intentions holy.

Nothing dries up the milk and honey of charity like regrets, afflictions, and melancholy. Live, then, in holy joy among those sons of our land. Give them a spiritual comfort kindly and graciously so that they may seek it gladly.

I am not telling you to fawn upon them, my dear Father, but be tender, mild, and amiable. In a word, love with a cordial, fatherly, and pastoral love these poor unfortunates of our times, and you will have done all; you will be all things to all men, a father to each one and helpful to all. This attitude alone is sufficient.

All Through the Day

Lord, make my heart simple and joyful, that I may love with your tenderness.

My Day Is Ending

Stay with me, Lord,
and teach me to live as a child before you,
trusting fully in your providence
and seeing your hand in all things.

Lord Jesus, you said,
"Unless you turn and become like children,
you will never enter the kingdom of heaven."
Help me to embrace that childlike simplicity
that brings joy to your heart.
Protect me from the weight of melancholy
and regrets that drain love from the soul.

Instead, fill me with holy joy,
that I may refresh others
and inspire them to seek you.

Grant me a heart of tenderness and love
toward those around me.

May I love not with flattery but with patience,
kindness, and sincerity so that I may reflect
your mercy and be all things to all people.
Amen.

DAY 19

My Day Begins

LETTER, JULY 7, 1913

Our Lord appeared and spoke to me as follows: "My son, do not fail to write down what you hear today from my lips so that you may not forget it. I am faithful, and no creature will be lost unwittingly. Light is very different from darkness. I invariably attract to myself a soul to whom I am accustomed to speak. On the contrary, the wiles of the devil tend to separate it from me. I never inspire in the soul any fears that drive it away from me; the devil never places in the soul any fears that induce it to draw near to me.

"If the fears the soul feels at certain moments of its life on the score of its eternal salvation proceed from me, they can be recognized by the peace and serenity they leave in the soul. . . ."

This vision and locution of Our Lord plunged my soul into such peace and happiness that all the sweetness of the world appears tasteless in comparison to even a single drop of this bliss.

Every fear concerning your own spiritual state vanished at once from my mind, and even though I attempted to doubt, I knew that such a doubt was not tenable. I am greatly comforted and very content in such good company. Who could describe the help it is to me to have Jesus continually by my side?

All Through the Day

Jesus, draw me close in peace and trust.

My Day Is Ending

Stay with me, Lord.
You speak to us with words
of truth and consolation.
You are faithful, and you never abandon a soul.
No one falls away from you by accident,
for your mercy always seeks and embraces us.

You draw souls with gentleness and love.
The enemy, by contrast, seeks to confuse us
with anxiety and unrest,

to separate us from the sweetness
of your presence.

Stay with me, Lord,
so I may taste the joy of your nearness,
a joy greater than all earthly sweetness.

Let this peace dissolve every doubt
and lead us to deeper trust.
Keep us always at your side,
where even a single drop of your love
makes us secure forever.

Amen.

DAY 20

My Day Begins

LETTER, NOVEMBER 1, 1913

My usual manner of praying is this: I no sooner begin to pray than my soul becomes enveloped in a peace and tranquility that words cannot describe. The senses become inactive . . . from this you will understand that I rarely succeed in using my mind in discursive prayer.

This state of soul is becoming so intense that it will be a miracle of Our Lord if I do not die of it. When the heavenly spouse of souls is pleased to put an end to this martyrdom, he suddenly sends me an irresistible spiritual fervor. In an instant everything is changed, and I feel so enriched by supernatural graces and so full of strength that I am ready to defy the whole of Satan's kingdom.

All I can say about this prayer is that my soul seems to be completely lost in God and that in those moments it gains more than it could in many years of intense spiritual exercises.

All this comes about not as a result of any consideration but by an interior flame and by such excessive love that if God did not come to my assistance, I should in a short time be burnt up.

All Through the Day

Enfold me in your peace, Lord, and consume me in your love.

My Day Is Ending

Stay with me, Lord,
when I turn to you in prayer;
enfold me in that peace beyond words,
where my restless thoughts fall silent
and my soul rests in your presence.

If your nearness overwhelms me,
let it be a holy martyrdom of love,
a sweetness so intense
that only your mercy sustains me.

Kindle in me a burning fervor,
filling me with strength, joy, and grace
so that no trial, no temptation,
can draw me away from you.

Lose me in yourself, O God,
for a single moment with you
is worth more than years of striving on my own.

Stay with me, Lord,
and let the interior flame of your love
consume all that is not of you,
until only your presence remains,
my strength, my joy, my everything.

Amen.

DAY 21

My Day Begins

LETTER, FEBRUARY 9, 1914

You asked me to give an account of my soul, and I regret that I am unable to explain myself because it is now a question of very lofty and secret things. Words are lacking by which to give even a feeble description of what passes between my soul and God in this state. The things that are taking place at present are so secret and private that anyone who has not himself experienced them could never, never form even a faint idea of them.

What my soul receives in this state is received in a very different manner from previously. It is now God himself who acts and operates directly in the depths of my soul without the ministry of the senses, either interior or exterior. This is, in a word, such a sublime, secret, and sweet operation that it is concealed from all human creatures and even from the intelligence of the rebellious angels.

All Through the Day

Lord, work in the secret places of my soul, where only your love reaches.

My Day Is Ending

Stay with me, Lord.
Your ways with the soul are higher
than words can ever reach.
What passes between you and the heart
lies beyond human language,
a mystery no mind can grasp,
a secret known only to you.

At times, prayer begins with thoughts, feelings,
or holy images,
but these are only stepping stones.
In the depths, you go beyond them all.
You act directly within the soul,
silently, tenderly, in ways unseen,
with a love that surpasses every effort of mine.

This is the grace of pure contemplation:
where I cease from striving and only receive,
while you yourself work in me,
planting seeds of eternal life,
watering them with hidden streams of grace.

Stay with me, Lord, and draw me ever deeper
into this hidden place,
where all words grow silent,
all fear and darkness vanish,
and only your light remains.
Let my soul rest in this secret union with you,
secure in the mystery of your love,
a love stronger than death,
a love eternal and unchanging.

Amen.

DAY 22

My Day Begins

LETTERS, SEPTEMBER 4, 1910

Jesus does not fail every now and then to mitigate my sufferings in another way, namely, by speaking within me. Oh, yes, my dear Father, how good Jesus is to me! What precious moments are these! This is a happiness for which I can find no comparison, a happiness that the Lord hardly ever allows me to taste except in the midst of suffering.

At such times more than any other, everything in this world wearies me and weighs upon me, and I desire nothing else than to love and to suffer. Yes, my dear Father, even in the midst of great sufferings, I feel happy, for I seem to feel my heart throbbing in unison with the heart of Jesus. Now you can imagine what a consolation it is to know almost with certainty that one possesses Jesus. . . .

It is also true that Jesus very often hides from me, but what does this matter? I shall always endeavor with your help to stay close to him, for you have assured me that this is not abandonment on his part but just the tricks of his love.

Oh, how much I longed to have someone to help me at such moments, to relieve my anxiety and moderate the flames that ravage my heart!

All Through the Day

Jesus, speak within me.

My Day Is Ending

Stay with me, Lord.
Even in the midst of suffering, you speak
within my soul,
and your presence brings a joy
beyond all comparison.

How sweet it is to feel my heart beating
in unison with yours,
sharing in both love and pain.
The world fades when I know you are near,
for my only desire is to love you
and to unite my sufferings with yours.

Yet at times you hide yourself,
and my soul feels the ache of longing.

Stay with me, Lord,
so that I will know these are not
signs of abandonment
but the tender ways of your love
drawing me deeper.
When the flames of love and sorrow grow heavy,
send your grace to sustain me
and let me rest in you.

Amen.

DAY 23

My Day Begins

LETTER, JUNE 28, 1912

Last night, I spent the entire night with Jesus in his Passion. I also suffered a great deal, but in a very different way from the previous night. This was a suffering that did me absolutely no harm. My trust in God increased more and more, and I felt increasingly attracted to Jesus. Although there was no fire nearby, I felt myself burning within; although there were no bonds, I felt myself tightly bound to Jesus. I burned with a thousand flames that made me live and die at the same time. Hence, I suffered, lived, and died continually.

Dear Father, if I could fly, I would like to shout, to cry out to everyone at the top of my voice, "Love Jesus, who is deserving of love."

All Through the Day

Jesus, bind me close in your burning love.

My Day Is Ending

Stay with me, Lord,
in the mystery of your Passion.

You draw my soul into a love that both
burns and consoles.
Here suffering is no longer
destruction but transformation,
a hidden fire that binds me to you more deeply
than words can say.

Though no chains restrain me, I feel held fast
in your embrace,
a bond of love stronger than death,
a union that makes my heart beat
in unison with yours.
Even in suffering, I am more alive,
for your love consumes me with a thousand flames,
a fire that wounds and heals,
that makes me die and live all at once.

Stay with me, Lord,
and let this burning love overflow beyond my soul.
Let every trial, every sorrow, become a song of praise
that cries out to the world:
Love Jesus, for he alone is worthy of love.
Take all that I am, Lord,
and transform my pain into intimacy,
my weakness into surrender,
my life into a flame of love for you.

May my voice, my breath, my very heartbeat
proclaim your goodness.
Grant that in joy or trial, in life or in death,
I may remain forever bound to you,
sharing in the mystery of your Cross,
and resting in the victory of your Resurrection.

Amen.

DAY 24

My Day Begins

LETTER, END OF JANUARY 1916

For some time past I have been plunged day and night into the dark night of the soul. My spiritual darkness lasts for long hours, long days, and frequently for entire weeks.

While I am immersed in this night of the soul, I cannot tell you whether I am in hell or in purgatory. The intervals in which a little light enters my soul are very brief, and while I am taking stock of my life, in a flash I fall into the dark prison. Immediately, then, all the favors the Lord has lavished on my soul are blotted out of my memory.

Farewell to the delight with which the Lord has inebriated my soul! Where is that enjoyment of adorable divine presence? Everything has disappeared from intellect and spirit; this is the native land of death, the night of abandonment, the cavern of desolation. Here the soul is far from its God and left to itself.

"My God, my God, why have you forsaken me?" (Mt 27:46, ESV). . . .

Torn away from its spouse, wounded in its inmost depths, my soul no longer knows what to do in this deepest night; and what increases my torment is the thought that these unbearable sufferings are to last forever, as it seems to me. My poor soul sees no end to this dreadful misery. It appears to me as if a metal wall has shut me into this horrible prison forever.

All Through the Day

Lord, in the darkness, I trust you.

My Day Is Ending

Stay with me, Lord.
In the depths of my soul,
I feel surrounded by darkness,
unable to perceive your presence.

My heart longs for the consolation and joy
I once knew,

yet now I feel abandoned, as if torn from you,
my divine Spouse.

Stay with me, Lord, and strengthen me
in this desolation.
Teach me to trust when feelings
of your nearness vanish.
Help me endure this trial
with faith and perseverance,
knowing that even in this "night,"
you are refining my soul.

Purify my attachments,
deepen my reliance on you,
and draw me ever closer.

Amen.

DAY 25

My Day Begins

LETTER, JULY 16, 1917

God is becoming ever more enlarged in my mind's eye, and I see him in the heavens of my soul surrounded by thick fog. I feel him near me, yet I see him quite far off. As my longing for him increases, he comes closer to me so that I feel him, yet my longing makes me see him farther and farther away. Dear God! How strange this is!

All Through the Day

Though God seems far away, he draws close.

My Day Is Ending

Stay with me, Lord,
so I can feel you within me
in the heavens of my soul,

and yet you are veiled, wrapped in the fog of mystery.
How can it be that I sense you here
and still reach for you as though you were far away?

The more I long for you, the more you come close.
Your nearness warms me, fills me,
and yet the same longing shows me
how infinite you are.
My desire grows, but so does the distance
that I cannot cross.
O sweet ache of the soul!
You make me hunger, and in the hunger I taste you.
You let me thirst, and in the thirst I drink of you.

O Lord,
you have become so vast in my heart
that I can no longer contain you.
You rise before me like the horizon,
endless, without limit,
and yet you draw near.

This strangeness is love itself.
For if I could seize you, you would no longer be God.

If I could measure you,
you would be less than infinite.
So you hide yourself in fog,
not to abandon me,
but to draw me onward,
deeper into your mystery,
where love is never finished, never exhausted.

O God of nearness, O God of distance,
teach me to rest in the paradox of your presence.
Let my longing for you never fade,
let my desire for you become my prayer,
until one day,
when the fog finally lifts,
I will see you face-to-face,
and the strangeness will be swallowed up in joy.

Amen.

DAY 26

My Day Begins

LETTER, SEPTEMBER 2, 1911

I also suffer greatly, Father, when I see how people ignore Jesus and, what is worse, how they even insult him, especially by those dreadful blasphemies. I should like to die or at least become deaf rather than hear so many insults offered to God by men.

I have prayed to the Lord as follows: Lord, let me die rather than be present when people are offending you!

All Through the Day

Jesus, I love you. Jesus, I adore you. Jesus,
I console your Heart.

My Day Is Ending

Stay with me, Lord.
You listened and forgave.

You bore blasphemy silently,
offering it to the Father.
Love does not flee from offense;
it transforms it into prayer, into mercy.

Stay with me, Lord.
Do not take me from this world too soon
but give me courage to remain in it
to hear the insults,
to bear them with you.
Let every blasphemy I hear invite me to whisper,
"Jesus, I love you. Jesus, I adore you.
Jesus, I trust in you."

O Heart of Jesus, so often wounded,
let me be a small consolation.
When others insult, let me bless.
When others scorn, let me kneel.
When others are indifferent, let me burn with love.

And if my longing becomes too heavy,
remind me: Even sorrow is your gift,
a share in your wounded love.

Jesus, give me strength to stay at your side,

until the day when all insults fall silent
and only love remains.

Amen.

DAY 27

My Day Begins

LETTER, JULY 1, 1915

Father, how sweet is the word *Cross*! Here at the foot of Jesus's Cross souls are clothed in light and inflamed with love; here they acquire wings to bear them upward in the loftiest flight.

May the same Cross always be our bed of rest, our school of perfection, our beloved heritage. For this reason, we must never separate the Cross from Jesus's love; otherwise, it would become a weight that, in our weakness, we could not carry.

May the Sorrowful Virgin obtain for us from her most holy Son the grace to penetrate more deeply into the mystery of the Cross and, like her, to become inebriated with Jesus's sufferings. The surest sign of love is the capacity to suffer for the beloved, and since the Son of God endured many sufferings for pure love, there is no doubt that the Cross carried for him becomes as lovable as love itself.

All Through the Day

At the foot of the Cross, I find light and love.

My Day Is Ending

Stay with me, Lord.
With you, the Cross becomes a treasure
where souls are clothed in light
and inflamed with love.
Left to myself, suffering feels meaningless,
but with you it becomes the place
where love is proven and redeemed.

The Cross is my teacher, my school of perfection.
Through it I am stripped of pride
and clothed in patience, humility, and compassion.
Each trial endured with you
teaches me to love more purely.

Holy Mary, Sorrowful Virgin,
you stood at the Cross with courage.
Teach me to remain as you did,
to embrace suffering with faith

and to trust that life flows even from pain
when it is united to Jesus.
You have shown that true love is proven in sacrifice.
May I prove my love for you
by carrying my daily crosses with patience.

Stay with me, Lord,
and teach me to love the Cross,
for in it I meet you.

Amen.

DAY 28

My Day Begins

LETTER, MAY 4, 1914

My soul seems determined to conspire against itself, making use of fantasy and imagination for this purpose. The beautiful days spent with the most sweet Jesus disappear completely from my mind. . . .

This state does not last long with the same intensity, nor could it last any longer, in my opinion, without separating my soul from the body. During this extreme trial, the highest point or apex of my soul is not disturbed in the least. . . .

This is a trial by fire, my dear Father, by a fire quite different from the fire of this base world. These two kinds of fire, however, have one thing in common, for both of them destroy and consume everything that places an obstacle in their way.

In point of fact, when my soul has come through this trial of fire, it is always more completely stripped of the vesture of the old man.

All Through the Day

Burn away my old self; clothe me in Christ.

My Day Is Ending

Stay with me, Lord.
My soul often seems divided against itself.
Memories of your sweetness fade,
and in their place come distractions,
fantasies, and storms of imagination
that make me feel far from you.

In these moments,
everything within me seems to burn.
It is a fire I cannot endure for long,
and yet, at the deepest part of my soul,
I sense a stillness untouched,
a secret place where I remain one with you.

This fire is not the fire of the world
but the fire of your love.
It consumes, it purifies,
and it burns away my pride,

my attachments, my illusions.
It strips me of the false self I cling to,
and though the pain is sharp,
I know you are clothing me anew in Christ.

Stay with me, Lord, and grant me courage
to remain in the flame until your work is done.
Let me not fear the burning,
for it is your hand that holds the fire.
And when I pass through it,
let me rise freer,
purer,
more wholly yours.

Amen.

DAY 29

My Day Begins

LETTER, MAY 1, 1912

Poor dear Mother, how you love me! I observed it once more at the dawn of this beautiful month. What great care she took to accompany me to the altar this morning. It seemed to me that she had nothing else to think about except me as she filled my whole heart with sentiments of holy love.

I felt a mysterious fire in my heart that I could not understand. I felt the need to put ice on it, to quench this fire that was consuming me.

I wish I had a voice strong enough to invite the sinners of the world to love Our Lady. But since this is not within my power, I have prayed and will pray to my dear Angel to perform this task for me.

All Through the Day

Jesus, increase my love for your Mother.

My Day Is Ending

Stay with me, Lord,
and through the flame of love,
may your Most Blessed Mother
lead my heart to yours and let my life be yours,
until at last I see the face of your Son
through your eyes of faith.

Fill my heart as you filled the heart of Padre Pio,
with that mysterious fire that consumes
all that is not of God.
Even when I cannot understand it,
let that flame purify me,
set me free,
and lift me closer to you.

O Blessed Mother,
tender and watchful,
you walk beside me as though I were your only child.
At the altar, you take my hand,
and in your gaze I feel the love of heaven itself.
Poor dear Mother, how you love me!

Teach me, O Mary,
to understand your ways,
your silence, your humility, your courage,
your constant yes to God.
Draw me into your life
so that I too may be clothed in your virtues
and burn with your fire of holy love.

Mother, I cannot call the world to love you
with my weak voice.
But I ask the angels
to carry this prayer to every soul:
Love Our Lady! Love her, and she will lead
you to Jesus.

Amen.

DAY 30

My Day Begins

LETTER, OCTOBER 24, 1913

What I understand most truly and clearly is that my heart loves to a much greater extent than my intellect perceives. Of this alone I am certain, and I have never had the slightest doubt about it. Moreover, I do not believe I am telling an untruth when I say that I have never been tempted in this respect. I am so perfectly sure that my will loves the most tender Spouse that, apart from the holy scripture, I am certain of nothing else to the same degree to which I am certain of this. . . .

In reciting the Lord's Prayer, before I pronounce the words "deliver us from evil," my whole soul is so taken up that, in spite of the efforts I make to restrain these movements, I feel myself carried away, as it were, into a different sphere, and I ask the heavenly Father to deliver me from every evil such as the present life. My soul understands, in a flash, that it can find no relief from its sufferings in this life, so far away from the immense good that is its beloved, and hence I ask the heavenly Father, with intense ardor, to set me free from the supreme evil that life represents for my soul and to admit me to the heavenly homeland close to my Beloved.

All Through the Day

Jesus, my heart loves you more than
I can understand.

My Day Is Ending

Stay with me, Lord.
My mind is small, my thoughts are weak,
but my heart loves you more than it can ever explain.
I do not understand all mysteries,
yet of this I am certain:
My soul loves you, my tender Spouse,
and nothing can shake that love.

When I pray, "Deliver us from evil,"
my soul longs not only for protection
but to be delivered from this exile of life,

where you feel so far away.
I ache for you, O Lord,
for nothing in this world can satisfy my heart.

Stay with me, Lord,
and teach me to love you with such
certainty and purity
that even my suffering becomes a longing for heaven.
Until that day when you bring me to yourself,
let my every prayer, my every breath,
be a whisper of love for you.

Amen.

Susan De Bartoli is the author of the award-winning *Welcoming the Christ Child with Padre Pio* and *Welcoming the Holy Spirit with Padre Pio*, as well as *Carry the Cross with Padre Pio*. She serves as the secretary of the Board of Directors of the Padre Pio Foundation of America and owns Little Flower Pilgrimages.

De Bartoli has been a guest on various radio and television shows and podcasts, including *Let Me Be Frank* with Bishop Frank J. Caggiano, *Seize the Day* with Gus Lloyd, EWTN's *Catholic Connection* with Teresa Tomeo, and Catholic Faith Network's *CFN Live*.

She is a lady commander of the Equestrian Order of the Holy Sepulchre of Jerusalem.

De Bartoli lives in the New York area.

littleflowerpilgrimages.com
Facebook: susan.debartoli
Instagram: @susan_debartoli